LAST MOMENT WITH DADDY

Jerquatta Jackson
Last moment with daddy

Published by BooxAi
ISBN: 978-965-578-979-9

LAST MOMENT WITH DADDY

JERQUATTA JACKSON

Last moment with daddy

I would like to dedicate this book to God, my father (Jerry blue) who is in Heaven, my amazing husband and beautiful family. To my siblings, and "Miss Cynthia Johnson" for believing in me, who, God allowed to birth the gift that is inside of me. I know she and my father are smiling at me.

I hope when you read this book, you are truly touched and feel renewed in Jesus's name, Amen!

Chapter 1

Why is it so hard to tell a loved one you're sick? Do you think it is going to hurt them more than you know? For a long time, I was so angry at my dad for not telling me. He tried to tell me, and I think in some of those moments I was too blind to see and hear.

I was sitting in the hospital room watching my dad, a lady enters the room, we exchanged a friendly greeting with one another, and my dad let her know that I was his daughter.

Her words lingered in my ear as she spoke to my father, **"I've been praying for you"! he replied, "thank you!"** In that moment confusion hit me as my thoughts began running in circles. **"Is he okay and why exactly is he here in the hospital?"** Everyone gathered in the room full of love, comfort, and genuine support because that is what my father was. It must have broken his heart to tell me he was dying in that hospital room. My heart was breaking at that moment because I did not know what he was facing or feeling inside.

One day I was watching TV and the lady said, **"you cannot cheat grief you got to go through the process of crying,**

feeling lonely, releasing the hurt, and relieving the pain," because one day it is going to get better.

After visiting with my dad, I told him I will be back to see him tomorrow. I had to prepare myself to be present at work the next day and get the kids ready for camp. Afterwards I found out my dad was leaving the hospital and heading to hospice, the confusion hit me again like, ***"what is going on with him?"*** I desperately needed more answers, and clarity.

Chapter 2

They said, ***"your dad took a turn!"*** I didn't even know my dad had stage four lung cancer. It was so heartbreaking, just imagining the agony and pain he was in during this time. Before I got off work, I got a phone call, the voice at the other end of the line said, ***"come to the hospice right now!"*** As I walked into that room, I saw some family members and then I looked at my dad. As I watched him lying in this condition, remembering the words ***"stage four lung cancer!"*** I could not utter a word, there was no talking, and the tears flowed from my eyes to my cheeks when I saw him, and I saw tears rolling from his eyes to his cheeks as well. At this time, I was 30 years old, and I've never seen my father cry. It felt like I was about to lose it! That moment was so heavy, only God knows how I truly felt! But it was there that I could feel God lifting me up with his perfect peace, even if I could not stand to see it or understand it. Peace was in the room.

The hospice had this distinct smell of death. It was an extremely large facility. Kids were kept on the second floor and the adults were on the third floor. To say the least, it broke my heart very much to watch my dad suffer in the pain he was in, and seeing him in this place, however it reminded me of Romans 8:18 (NKJV) "For I consider that the sufferings of this present time are not worthy to be compared with the glory that shall be revealed in us." My dad's suffering was God's plan, so that I can truly see the glory of God.

That was the clarity and reassurance I needed. Knowing God was getting me through this season. My dad was never alone, there was always someone in his room, whether it was a nurse or family member. One night after a hospice visit to see my dad. My husband and I had just walked through the door, and my phone began to ring. I answered the phone and the person on the other end said, ***"come back your dad is not going to make it."*** I rushed to the hospice with my husband, Anthony, so many thoughts were running through my head. When we arrived, I immediately went to my dad's room. It was surreal watching his heartbeat on the monitor, as his body was shutting down, his heart rhythm faded. I'm a sensitive person, my emotions were on a roller coaster, going up and down. There was fear creeping inside of me, from seeing all the doctors and nurses, to thinking about every patient that is lying on their deathbed. I just sensed so much, and I had to run down the hall and catch a breath before I fainted. I felt so overwhelmed at that moment.

That Friday, I had plans to go celebrate my birthday, but I had so much sadness going on thinking about my dad. Even though my dad was sick, I knew he would have wanted me to celebrate my birthday. My husband decided to take me to New York. My sister-in-law, along with my brother-in-law. My birthday weekend was incredibly beautiful, I tried my best to enjoy it, but I really could not enjoy it. It was like putting on a fake smile, I was present for the love around me, but sadness was taking over tremendously. I thought I was strong enough to be around other people. Deep down inside I really was not strong at all. My sister brought me a cake and I was so appreciative of her, and till this day I have kept the cake in my freezer. It is a keepsake, and I hold on to it so that I will not forget.

Where do you find peace in a situation like this? I didn't have the answers, but I knew God was with me. I had mixed emotions, sadness, crying, even joy that I knew he was going to be with the Lord, but I was strong because I knew God was with me and my dad. I went downstairs, I left the room and as I got off the elevator to my left, I noticed a picture. The picture was of a woman standing strong, her chin was up, she was trying to cross the bridge, but the bridge was broken and looked difficult to cross. At that moment, the Holy Spirit spoke to me and said ***"Do you trust me, are you scared to cross that bridge? I am with you."***

I did not understand at the time. I was looking at the picture and asking myself, how would I cross that bridge? But the Lord had my back, he knew what was about to happen. I just had to breathe because this was my last moment with my dad. The tuxedo that my dad walked me down the aisle in was the same tuxedo I buried him in. On the day of the funeral, it was marvelous, in the same aspect of how he loved me. He looked nice and at the time, I didn't have an emotional breakdown. I was handling my emotions well. Family and friends told me **"You'll go through different emotional stages when someone you love dies."**

When my dad passed, I went through stages thinking he was still alive. I went through stages of crying, but it was that one Sunday my Pastor was preaching, I could feel it in my heart. It felt so heavy and one of the ministers came to meet me at the altar, someone grabbed my hand and brought me to the altar, it was The Lord. He grabbed my hand and that was it. I broke loose and gave it all to Him. I could not keep being strong anymore for anyone! I got my breakthrough there. I fell to my knees and said God, help me. Nobody noticed I was trying to be strong! I was trying to be strong for my sister, I was trying to be strong for my brother's, and I was trying to be strong for my father's family. I realized I was weak, my heart had to heal. Everything is possible with God if you trust in Him, and I knew that in God's time my heart would heal and be restored.

ked by d   d **5 others**

jcblue1988 Proverbs 31 verse 25-26 strength and honor are her clothing; she shall rejoice in time to come she open her mouth with wisdom. And on her tongue is the law of kindness.

Matthew 11:28 "Come to me, all who are weary and heavily burdened, and I will give you rest." Now I am the one facing the water, saying does it get worse or better after this. I trust you Lord, but I do not understand this season. The staff at the hospice center continued to send me information about their grief classes. I never went. I knew it would be helpful to talk about the situation, however God was dealing with me during this time. Prayer always worked and crying it out did too. I am not sure if grief will get better, but there is peace on the other side and better days ahead.

"For this reason, I remind you to fan into flame the gift of God, which is in you through the laying on of my hands." 2 Timothy 1:6 NIV

The hands of my dad and me.

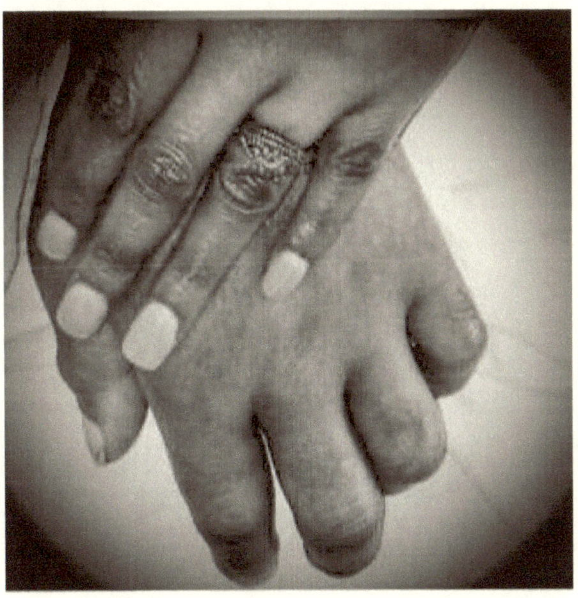

My dad informed me that my sister was coming to town, and he wanted us to meet and take pictures. I remember it like it was yesterday, it was on a Sunday, I went to my dad's house after church. My sister came over and I met my niece and nephews, I

was happy to see them. We took pictures together with my children and dad, the joy on his face, only the Lord knew that made his day, it was the best day especially to see his girls together.

For the first time, looking back now in his mind, he knew he was about to be with the Lord, I could tell because he had so much peace. I could see that with my own eyes even when we took pictures together. So much of that day reminded me of the scripture 1 Corinthians 13:13 *"And now these three remain; faith hope and love. but the greatest of these is love."* Love was in that room; this was the beginning of our last moments with dad.

We are smiling, we have peace! John 14:27 *"Peace I leave with you; My peace I give to you, I do not give to you as the world gives. Do not let your heart be troubled and do not be afraid."*

Visiting my dad's grave site…

The pain

The doctor asked me if I knew anybody that smoked cigars, if so, I should advise them to stop because lung cancer is very painful, it breaks down your body so fast making it difficult to eat.

Here are some signs and symptoms of early lung cancer, as my dad went through all these symptoms.

- A cough that will not go away or a so-called "smoker's cough" that sounds raspy
- Coughs that produce blood or rust-colored phlegm
- Hoarseness; trouble breathing or noisy breathing
- Shortness of breath or wheezing
- Loss of appetite and weight loss
- Chest pain gets worse when you cough or breathe deeply

Every time I went to see my dad in hospice, he was never alone, he always had company coming to see him, friends, and family, he was very loved. I would often sit in the chair next to him saying to myself, "this can't be real." Dad was not in pain at hospice, he was on so much medication that his body started swelling from it. They were just doing their job, you know why the hospice visit was sad, my dad was on the second floor and on the 3 floors were little kids, doing the same thing. You can feel all the pain in that building, I wonder if the staff ever get used to it or it does not bother them. The smell of death is not a good.

It was a beautiful sunny summer day, the sun was shining, I was just getting off work ready to head home after a long day. My phone began to ring and to my surprise, it was my dad. I answered the phone and Dad said, "Come see me."

He told me he was in the hospital. I really did not think anything of it, so, I went up to the hospital to see him. When I arrived and walked into the room, I saw 3 family members and my dad who was happy and smiling to see me. I knew he was sick, but I did not think it was that bad, I did not think this would be the last moment that I was going to see him. At that moment that's when life hit hard for my family. I stayed for a little while at the hospital. I observed nurses coming back and forth checking on him. During that time, we were hanging around telling jokes, laughing, talking and then, I felt it, there was this sadness in the room it was as if I could feel everyone's emotions that were permeating in dads room there was a nurse that came in to see my dad she told him I'm praying for you then she left with a look of sadness on her face. Many people do not like hospitals, the smell, the fear, it is a lot of emotions, the lady that came in the room to see my dad introduced me to her she said hi this is my daughter. I still did not think anything of it so I kissed him on the cheek, and I told him I will see him tomorrow before I left, I suggested that we call my sister, so I called her on my phone and we FaceTime. My sister and my dad talked; she also did not think that would be the last moment she would hear his voice. Did I mention we are Daddy's Little Girls! The next day I called him, but he really could not talk over the phone. The pain was so uncomfortable for him to speak. I asked him if he was going to be ok, he said yes, he is going back home in a couple more days. I ask myself... how could I have been so blind not knowing my dad was this sick? He did not think I would be strong enough to take the pain or did he think I was weak? The next day I went to see him they transferred him to a hospice. My dad wanted to go home but my family member suggested that it was best for him to stay at the hospice. Dad looked so tired you could almost tell that he was giving up. I sat at the edge of his bed, he closed his eyes and told all the family members, "I'm going to be ok," that was the last words I heard my dad say. I got a phone call from my sister; she was in town. I picked her up and we went to see dad. When we arrived at the hospice dad was asleep. He never opened his eyes back up. It was great to see my sister, especially during a time like this. She is my older sister, and she has three beautiful kids. My dad always talked about her, and little did we know the last moment with my dad our family was about to feel our heart shatter into pieces.

Is this really my life day 3 his body?

Genesis 2:15

The LORD God took the man and put him in the Garden of Eden to work it and take care of it. He works ever Singel day got up every morning you could not stop him.

Jerry Louis Blue

When my dad would call my phone, he would always ask me to bring the kids over so he could see them. If I knew the condition he was in before he went to the hospital, he would have seen them every day! I really did not know and on some days I feel sad. That Friday, I had plans to go celebrate my birthday, but I felt bad. I know my dad was sick, but I also knew he wanted me to celebrate my birthday. My husband decided to take me to New York. My sister-in-law, along with my brother-in-law were there. My birthday weekend was beautiful, I tried my best to enjoy it, but I really could not enjoy it, it was like putting on a fake smile. I thought I was strong enough to be around other people, well at least I thought I was, did I mention my sister bought me a cake, and I still have the cake to this day in my freezer. I wanted it to be a memory forever.

I thought, where do you find peace in a situation like this? I am sure the Lord was with me. I had mixed emotions, sadness, crying, even joy that I knew he was going to be with the Lord, but was I being strong because I knew the Lord? I went downstairs, I left the room and as I got off the elevator to my left, I noticed a picture. The picture was of a woman standing strong, her chin was up, she was trying to cross the bridge, but the bridge was broken and looked difficult to cross. At that moment, the Holy Spirit spoke to me and said "Do you trust me, are you scared to cross that bridge? I am with you."

I did not understand at the time. I was looking at the picture and asking myself, how would I cross that bridge? But the Lord had my back, He knew what was about to happen. I just had to breathe because this was my last moment with my dad. The Tuxedo that my dad walked me down the aisle in was the same tuxedo I buried him in. On the day of the funeral, it was nice. He looked nice and at the time, I did not have any type of emotional breakdown. I was handling my emotions well. Family and friends assured me that you go through different emotional stages when someone dies that you love.

When my dad passed, I went through stages thinking he was still alive. I went through stages of crying, but it was that one Sunday my Pastor was preaching, I could feel it in my heart. It felt so heavy and one of the ministers came to meet me at the altar, someone grabbed my hand and brought me to the altar, it was The Lord.

He grabbed my hand and that was it. I broke loose and gave it all to Him. I could not keep being strong anymore for anyone! I got my breakthrough there. I fell to my knees and said God, help me. Nobody noticed I was trying to be strong! I was trying to be strong for my sister, I was trying to be strong for my brother's, and I was trying to be strong for my father's family. I realized I was weak, my heart had to heal overtime. Everything is possible with God if you trust in Him. completely shut down, as I was leaving work, they called me. I ran to the room and cried. Seeing him lying down, tears just continued to roll down his face seeing my brother break down, that was his friend. He did everything with him, family members were crying too. I was still lost because I did not understand what happened. I knew he had lung cancer, but no one told me that he was in his last stage, he did not even tell me. I was angry with him because I was trying to understand.

I had to pray and ask God to help me with this, because my mind was everywhere. They say that the last functioning mechanism on a person's body before death is their ears. I could not help but imagine how dad felt hearing the crying, the pain of his kids? The Lord had to help me with this. I texted a few people from my church and told them to pray for my family, especially my siblings. Have you ever smelled death? Well, I did. We stayed in his room all day to be with him by his side then one of the nurses came in to give us a booklet and told us to read.

This and inside it was telling us what to expect in these last moments. I was really lost saying to myself "why she's giving us a booklet on death?" No one told me this was about to happen. Our dad's last time with us, I never experienced anything like this. stages of your body about to shut down before you are about to die. This cannot really be happening. I was waiting for my dad to wake up out of this, because some people do wake up out of this. We were not so blessed at that time, but I knew he was at peace. In my dad's file he said he did not want restoration, he was okay. The Nurse said to me that my dad was a fighter in the condition he was in. He was a strong man just like how he was when he was on this Earth. Dad worked every single day; he never took any days off work.

So, as I sat with him on the side of his bed he looked as if he was just sleeping in. I was so sad now because my birthday was in two days, and he knew my birthday was coming up. He was fighting to stay alive; he did not want to die on my birthday, I know that for sure. I was thinking to myself, is this about to happen? Am I about to see someone go away for a long time and never come back in my heart? I know he is with Jesus and his mother. In heaven smiling down. I am keeping my dad alive sharing the memory of him. I was at the gas station getting ready to go to work and I got a phone call from the hospice. I picked up the phone and that is when she told me Jerry Blue had just passed away. My heart dropped, I jumped in the car and dropped the kids off. I grabbed my sister, sister Jasmine and my mother. We were on our way, and I felt like I was driving in a circle. For some reason, I could not get to the site where my husband was working that day. I was in panic mode I knew I would feel the last moment. We finally got to the hospice. It felt like an hour to get there even though it only took 10 minutes. I walked into the room; I saw tears coming down dad's face, but the room was so peaceful. He was at peace, it looked like he was just sleeping in the bed, his skin was so warm that I touched him. I gave him a kiss on the forehead like he always used to do to me. I was numb because this was the last moment, I would get to touch my dad. I beat myself up that night, I should have stayed the night with him at hospice, because that morning he died. Why wasn't I by his side? I thought back to that night that I had a dream about my dad and the Lord said, He's taking him home, that dream was so amazing. I know I had the peace of the Lord with me because of my church family's prayers. Th dream was Jesus and my dad he dah him by the hand. It was a Sunday morning; I was at church. I fell to my knees and angels were surrounding me with the love of God. Something that was broken was pulled out at that altar. I felt peace at that very moment. A couple of days later, I started going through the stages. I thought he was still alive! I cried every day! I had to find out on my own how to cope with this loss. It never gets easy, but it gets better especially when you walk with the Lord. He will help you, I had to trust the Lord. and I had a couple of days after my dad passed. The Lord touched my heart; He healed my mind, yet I continued to feel myself going into a deep depression. That Sunday morning at the altar, I give it all to God and I just needed that touch from God. My church family prayed for me and my family. When you have support when you go through a tragedy like this, you need people that are going to be there for you. This is my story. This is the last moment I was with my dad. Proverbs 3 verse 5 Trust in the Lord with all your heart and lean not on your own understanding. I am so glad I did not go by my own understanding with this. If I did, can you imagine how angry I would have been blaming everybody because of my dad but the Lord gives strength to his children, he said my breakthrough is bigger than your thoughts. Thank you, Jesus with the Holy Spirit, thanks for leading me in the right direction. I miss my dad, he is in a better place now, we will meet again. About 1 years before my dad tried to tell me he had lung cancer, and it never came out of his mouth. I had to find out by my brothers that he was sick he thought he was trying For to same me I knew something was wrong I was praying for him my church had a healing night and the next day I bring him a prayer cloth I told him out to put it in his wallet when we was cleaning out his apartment I found the prayer cloth I Believe In My Heart that God heal some wounds that was broken inside of him some forgiveness yes he passed from lung cancer but he was a fighter my dad was sad he really miss his mother when she pass that tore him up in my heart I believe they are seeing each and celebrate with Jesus my dad wear some black and blue sneakers to the hospital. That's the only thing I have left of him people ask me why I still have them I feel as his I keep the shoes because the journey he walks in these shoes when he had lung cancer, he fought the good fight when I look at the sneakered was not scared to face what was in front on him that's moving on to light. He walked in a hospital knowing that he was not able to walk back out.so he moves on.im at peace. My dad died 3 days later he knew my Birthday was coming up and, in his heart, he knew time was running out and he was ok with that. He a strong man that love his kids.

The picture we took in hospice my sister and brother we were next to my dad at his bedside.

What a blessing for him to see this day

Me and my dad on my wedding day, can you imagine he was in pain on this day, and I did not know.

Me and my dad on my wedding day, can you imagine, he was in pain on this day, and I did not know.

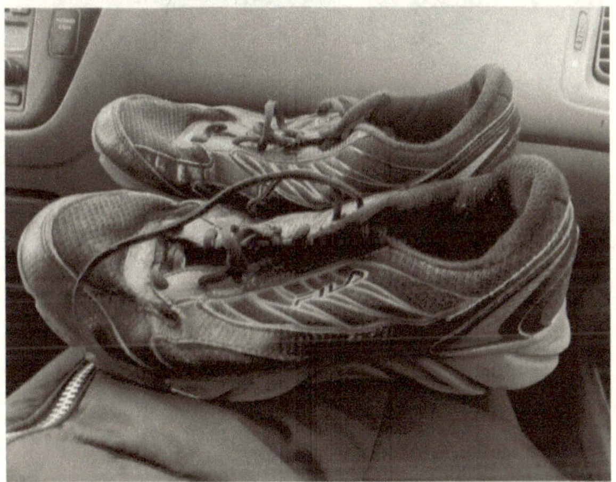

When I was getting on the elevator I look to my right and seen

This beautiful picture at hospice and I was standing just like her
with my hands on my hips. And that's when the holy spirit spoke
to me and said look deepen at this picture don't be afraid your
dad is about to be with me you have to cross the bright I know it
look scary and booking pierce and look dark the lord said trust

me I'm with you the lord said I know you looking over the bright and you see the end broking. Do not worry about the light over there. It is not going to be easy I promise it is going to be worth it. I cried because I did not understand until 2 years later to author this book of my story help other people who lose their dad. From lung cancer you are going to help get them through your testimony how the lord got you throw and the saint prayer. Can I mention prayer always works no matter the situation?

NAME: **Jerry L. Blue**
BIRTH: **15 Jan 1959**
DEATH: **18 Jul 2016**

Before my dad does a job, he always writes the vision down before he does it. Multiple pens on his little table on his table in his kitchen brown old wooden table everything plan in at the table my dad knew he was dying cause the doctor told him the chemo was not working anymore I find that. He wrote a letter to his kids he loves to write. I will never know but in my heart, he did that true. The hospital visits and hospice were different, he was talking alert in the hospital and laughing and smiling. hospice that is when he never came out, I said this my dad was firm believe know where you are going when you died my dad was save, I know he in a heaven I love the 3 HHH hospital hospice heaven what a journey right they said everything come in 3.

Completely shut down, as I was leaving work, they called me. I ran to the room and cried. Seeing him lying down, tears just continued to roll down his face seeing my brother break down, that was his friend. He did everything with him, family members were crying too. I was still lost because I did not understand what happened. I knew he had lung cancer, but no one told me that he was in his last stage, he did not even tell me. I was angry with him because I was trying to understand.

I had to pray and ask God to help me with this, because my mind was everywhere. They say that the last functioning mechanism on a person's body before death is their ears. I could not help but imagine how dad felt hearing the crying, the pain of his kids? The Lord had to help me with this. I texted a few people from my church and told them to pray for my family, especially my siblings. Have you ever smelled death? Well, I did. We stayed in his room all day to be with him by his side then one of the nurses came in to give us a booklet and told us to read this and inside it was telling us what to expect in these last moments. I was really lost saying to myself "why she's giving us a booklet on death?" No one told me this was about to happen. Our dad's last time with us, I never experienced anything like this.

Stages of your body about to shut down before you are about to die. This cannot really be happening. I was waiting for my dad to wake up out of this, because some people do wake up out of this. We were not so blessed at that time, but I knew he was at peace. In my dad's file he said he did not want restoration, he was okay.

The Nurse said to me that my dad was a fighter in the condition he was in. He was a strong man just like how he was when he was on this Earth. Dad worked every single day; he never took any days off work.

So, as I sat with him on the side of his bed he looked as if he was just sleeping in. I was so sad now because my birthday was in two days, and he knew my birthday was coming up. He was fighting to stay alive; he did not want to die on my birthday, I know that for sure.

I was thinking to myself, is this about to happen? Am I about to see someone go away for a long time and never come back in my heart? I know he is with Jesus and his mother.

In heaven smiling down I am keeping my dad alive sharing the memory of him.

Was at the gas station getting ready to go to work and I got a phone call from the hospice. I picked up the phone, that is when she told me Jerry Blue had just passed away. My heart dropped, I jumped in the car and dropped the kids off. I grabbed my sister, sister Jasmine and my mother. We were on our way, and I felt like I was driving in circles. For some reason, I could not get to the site where my husband was working that day. I was in panic mode I knew I would feel the last moment.

We finally got to the hospice. It felt like an hour to get there even though it only took 10 minutes. I walked into the room; I saw tears coming down dad's face, but the room was so peaceful. He was at peace, it looked like he was just sleeping in the bed, his skin was so warm that I touched him. I gave him a kiss on the forehead like he always used to do to me. I was numb because this was the last moment, I would get to touch my dad.

I beat myself up that night, I should have stayed the night with him at hospice, because that morning he died. Why wasn't I by his side? I thought back to that night that I had a dream about my dad and the Lord said, He's taking him home, that dream was so amazing. I know I had the peace of the Lord with me because of my church family's prayers. Th dream was Jesus and my dad he dah him by the hand.

It was a Sunday morning; I was at church. I fell to my knees and angels

This is my story this is the last moment I was with my dad….

Proverbs 3 verse 5 Trust in the Lord with all your heart and lean not on your own understanding.

I am so glad I did not go by my own understanding with this. If I did, can you imagine how angry I would have been blaming everybody because of my dad but the Lord gives strength to his children, he said my breakthrough is bigger than your thoughts. Thank you, Jesus with the Holy Spirit, thanks for leading me in the right direction.

I miss my dad; he is in a better place now. We will meet again.

About 1 years before my dad tried to tell me he had lung cancer, and it never came out of his mouth. I had to find out by my brothers that he was sick he thought he was tr8ying For to same me I knew something was wrong I was praying for him my church had a healing night and the next day I bring him a prayer cloth I told him to put it in his wallet when we was cleaning out his apartment I found the prayer cloth I Believe In My Heart that God heal some wounds that was broken inside of him some forgiveness yes he passed from lung cancer but he was a fighter my dad was sad he really miss his mother when she pass that tore him up in my heart I believe they are seeing each and celebrate with Jesus my dad wear some black and blue sneakers to the hospital.

That's the only thing I have left of him people ask me why I still have them I feel as his I keep the shoes because the journey he walks in these shoes when he had lung cancer, he fought the good fight when I look at the sneaker, he was not scared to face what was in front on him that's moving on to light. He walked in a hospital knowing that he was not able to walk back out.so he moves on.im at peace.

My dad died 3 days later he knew my Birthday was coming up and, in his heart, he knew time was running out and he was ok with that. He a strong man that love his kids.

Jerquatta Jackson is an author, mother loving wife & prayer warrior. Passionate in helping women reach their spiritual salvation and to know the Lord and fulfil their ultimate purpose in life. Ministry bloom and prayer it is a prayer ministry.

Email: Jcblue1988@gmail